All golfing fees with the compliments of:
Angelic Airlines

This book belongs to:

....

From:

....

Date:

....

Signed by:

My First Fun Golf Steps

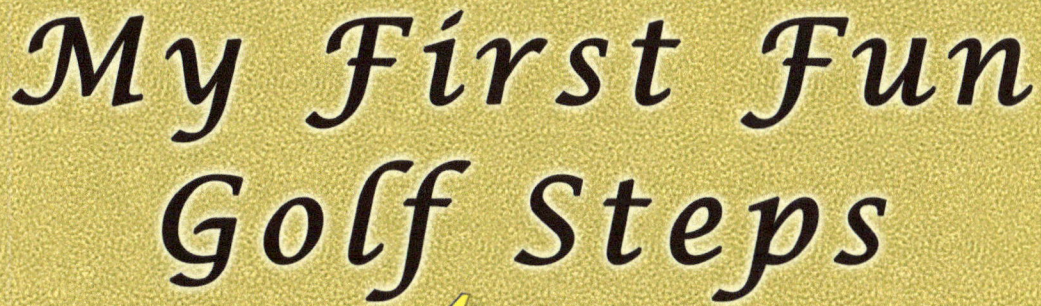

John Othitis

My First Fun Golf Steps - Authored by John G. Othitis

No part of this publication may be reproduced, stored in a retrieval   system or transmitted in anyway by any means, electronic, mechanical, photocopy, and recording. With intend only to be used for personal reasons. Not to be amended, distributed, sell, quote, use any part of the content within this book without the prior permission of the author except as provided by the USA copyright law.

Copyright © 2014 John G. Othitis

Illustrated by Holly Sellors

All rights reserved.

ISBN-13: 978-1-910115-14-5

Cover design, Editing and Formatting by LionheART Publishing House, part of LionheART Galleries Ltd

Dedicated
to my amazing parents
who supported me throughout my
junior golfing years

Acknowledgements

Mr. Doug Matthews; a great person for his guidance and encouragement, and Graeme Matthews, my school and golfing friend. They introduced me to my first golfing game at the Gweru Golf Club. In no time I was playing golf in local and national junior and senior golf club competitions locally and nationwide. Nomads 21, Zimbabwe Junior Golf team, PE Technikon College, RSA teams and more.

MEET THE KANNUKA TEAM

Roary the Lion

MEET THE KANNUKA TEAM

Sahara the Elephant

MEET THE KANNUKA TEAM

Chips the Monkey

MEET THE
KANNUKA TEAM

Zazzi the Leopard

What We Need to Know About the Game of Golf

Golf Club   Golf Putter

Golf Wood

What we Need to Know About the Game of Golf

Divot

Golf Bag

Tee Box

THIS IS A:

Putting Green and Flag Stick

Bunker

Golf Ball on a Tee

THIS IS A:

Putting Green

Golf Hole

Always Make Sure
You Are Prepared
Before A Golf Game

That you have tees and golf balls . . .

. . . in your golf bag

Get ready, Roary

is going to play

off the tee box

SAFETY

Golf clubs are made of hard metal and can be dangerous when swinging.

Chips stands at a safe
distance when Roary hits
the golf ball
with his golf club.

Look Ahead Before You Hit the Ball

Be Very Cautious

Roary does not hit the golf ball if there are other players in front of him

Kalu is holding the flag pole.

RESPECT

The green on the golf course can be easy to damage.

Kalu takes extra care when walking on the green

Kalu also makes sure not to drag his feet and Putter on the green.

SHHHH . . . NO NOISE
STAY QUIET

Sahara makes sure

To stay quiet

when it is Lily's

turn to hit the golf ball.

Be Careful In The Rough Grass

Chips has hit the golf ball off the fairway

He has to try and hit the ball from the rough grass back onto the fairway. He has to be careful he does not hit the tree with his golf club.

MANNERS

Lily is in the bunker

Lily makes sure to

RAKE the sand after her bunker shot

This keeps the sand nice and smooth for other players it is good manners and respect.

Zazzi is about to putt on the green

PATIENCE

Zazzi's golf ball is the furthest from the hole. She will putt her golf ball first towards the hole.

Kalu will hold the flag stick for Zazzi.

Roary, Chips, Kalu, Lily, Sahara and Zazzi.

Thank you to all our Kannuka friends from Africa for playing golf with Johnny

They love to play golf and will see you
soon to show you more golf tips and
more sports to play with me.

We thank Captain Frankie
and his Angelic Airlines
for flying us to Zimbabwe, Africa
where we enjoyed our first golf lesson
with our favorite animals.

"GOLF IS SUCH GREAT FUN"

See you soon with more golfing fun and
tips for you to improve your golf.
Thank you for visiting our
Kannuka Golf Club!

About the Author and Golfer:

John G. Othitis started playing golf from the early age of eight years old, spending many hours on the golf course. He played in many junior golfing competitions representing his local town, and won many major Junior and Senior competitions for the Gweru Golf Club, Zimbabwe, Africa.

He pursued his love of Golf in Port Elizabeth, South Africa, where he attended University, and continued to represent his team.

John majored in Sports and Marketing. To this day, John continues to play Golf in Canada where he enjoys teaching young children his passion: golf. His deepest love is working with the special needs children.

Get your Friends to Sign Your Own Fan Page

www.ingramcontent.com/pod-product-compliance
Lightning Source LLC
Chambersburg PA
CBHW041744040426
42444CB00001B/26